T0059131

Sing Low

Sacred music for lower voices

Selected & edited by Barry Rose

Front cover photograph of Gloucester Cathedral by
courtesy of Rex Features.
Back cover photograph of Barry Rose by Timothy Hands.
Cover designed by Michael Bell Design.
Music setting by Stave Origination.

NOV 381000
ISBN 0-7119-9232-0

© Copyright 2002 Novello & Company Limited.
Published in Great Britain by Novello Publishing Limited.

Head Office
14/15 Berners Street, London W1T 3LJ, England.
Telephone: +44 (0)20 7434 0066
Fax: +44 (0)20 7287 6329

Exclusive distributors:
Hal Leonard Europe Limited
Distribution Centre
Newmarket Road, Bury St Edmunds Suffolk, IP33 3YB
www.halleonard.com

www.chesternovello.com
All Rights reserved.
Printed in EU.

We have endeavoured to trace all copyright holders but we
will be pleased to rectify in future reprints any omissions notified to us.

No part of this publication may be copied or
reproduced in any form or by any means without the
prior permission of Novello Publishing Limited.

Foreword

Although much of the usual repertoire for choirs is scored for SATB, part of the brief for the New Novello Choral Programme is to provide for other combinations of voices, and to this end we have already published two volumes for high voices – *High Praise* (NOV 032118) and *Merrily on High* (NOV 032121).

Now we welcome you to *Sing Low*, a comprehensive collection of anthems, motets, settings and responses originally scored, or specially transposed for lower voices. This long-awaited selection, made in response to many requests from choir directors, is the first such volume to be published for over 30 years. The contents cover many aspects of the liturgical year, offering a rich resource of new and previously unpublished compositions from distinguished musicians of today coupled with material drawn from archives.

In researching, editing and selecting the 29 pieces contained here, I have been greatly assisted by my fellow choral advisors, Ralph Allwood, David Hill and Brian Kay, and am also grateful to Howard Friend at Novello & Co. and to Elizabeth Robinson for her untiring care and patience in the preparation and publication of this volume.

Barry Rose *Somerset, June 2002*

Sing Low

Sacred music for lower voices

Selected & edited by Barry Rose

Ave Maria (Angelus Domini)

Text from Luke I, John I and Pius X

Franz Biebl

© 1964 by Wildt's Musikverlag, Dortmund

ple - na, Do - mi - nus te - cum, be - ne -

-na, Do - mi - nus te - cum, be - ne - di - cta

- di - cta tu in mu - li - e - ri -

tu_____ in mu - li - e - ri - bus

(repeat Ave Maria)

(2) Plainsong
TENOR 1 SOLO

Et ver - bum ca - ro fac - tum est

(2)

et ha - bi - ta - vit___ in no - bis.

(repeat Ave Maria)

- sus. San - cta Ma - ri - a, ma - ter___

- sus. San - cta Ma - ri - a, ma - ter De - i,

De - i, o - ra pro no - bis pec - ca - to - - ri -

o - ra pro no - bis pec - ca - to - - ri - bus.

If sung a semitone higher, the top line of Choirs I and II may be doubled by Altos.

The original version was written for Julian Lambart and the Eton College Lower Chapel Choir

Behold now, praise the Lord

Psalm 134

William H. Harris

An arrangement of the anthem for upper voices published in 'High Praise', NOV 032118

© Copyright 1961 Novello & Company Limited

sanc - tua-ry, and praise the Lord.

and praise the Lord.

praise the Lord. The Lord that made

The Lord that made heav'n and

The Lord that made heav'n and

heav'n and earth,

earth, made heav'n and earth

earth, made heav'n and earth give thee

made heav'n and earth

Sw.

Gt. to
Ped. in

Gt. to Ped.

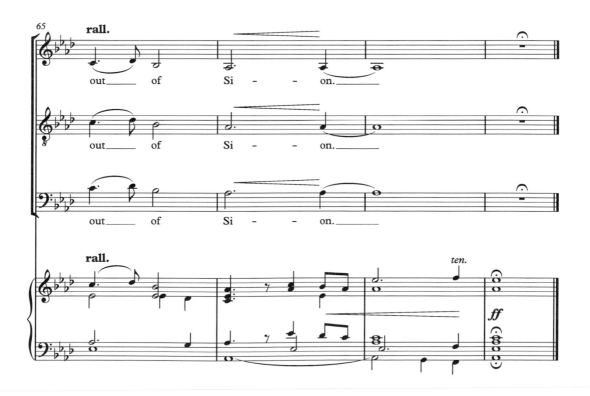

For Bryan Hesford

By the waters of Babylon

Psalm 137, vv.1-4

Arthur Wills

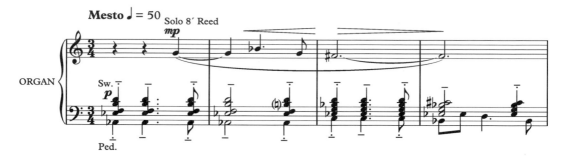

© Copyright 1966 Novello & Company Limited

when we re-mem-bered thee, O Si-on.

As for our harps, we hanged them up: up-on the

trees that are there-in.

For

when we re-mem-bered thee,

when we re-mem-bered thee,

when we re-mem-bered thee,

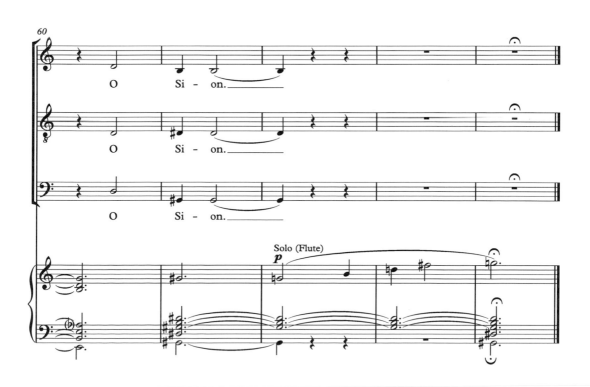

O Si - on.

O Si - on.

O Si - on.

Solo (Flute)

To Gillie and Frank

Christ hath a garden

Isaac Watts

Jeremy Jackman

© Copyright 2002 Novello & Company Limited

A -mong the trees that he hath set,

A -mong the trees__ that he hath set,

TUTTI
SOLO

yet, A -mong the trees that he hath set, That he may e - ver -more be

To walk a - mid the spring - ing,__ spring - ing__ green.

To walk a - mid the spring - ing,____ spring - ing____ green.

TUTTI

seen. To walk a - mid the spring - ing, spring - ing green.

For Barry Rose and the Gentlemen of St. Albans Abbey Choir

Come, thou Redeemer of the earth

St. Ambrose,
tr. J.M. Neale and others

Melody adapted by Michael Praetorius
arr. Andrew Parnell

© Copyright 2002 Novello & Company Limited

32′ St. Albans, October 1991, rev. May 2001

Exsultate justi

Psalm 33, vv.1-3

Ludovico da Viadana
ed. Anthony G. Petti

© Copyright 1977 J. & W. Chester/Edition Wilhelm Hansen London Ltd.
This edition © Copyright 2002 Chester Music Limited

Let the just rejoice in the Lord: it is fitting for the upright to praise him.
Sing to him to the psaltery and the ten-stringed lute. Make him a new song:
sing to him well with strong voice.

Give rest, O Christ

tr. W.J. Birkbeck

Kiev melody
ed. Walter Parratt

The note values are relative rather than actual, and the rhythm should depend largely on the verbal accent, as in plainsong.
The music should be sung with much fervour.

This arrangement may be sung by ATTB, a tone higher.

© Copyright 1915 Novello & Company Limited

To Dr. Basil Harwood

God so loved the world

John 3, vv.16-17

Henry G. Ley

© Copyright 1911 Stainer & Bell Ltd., London, England

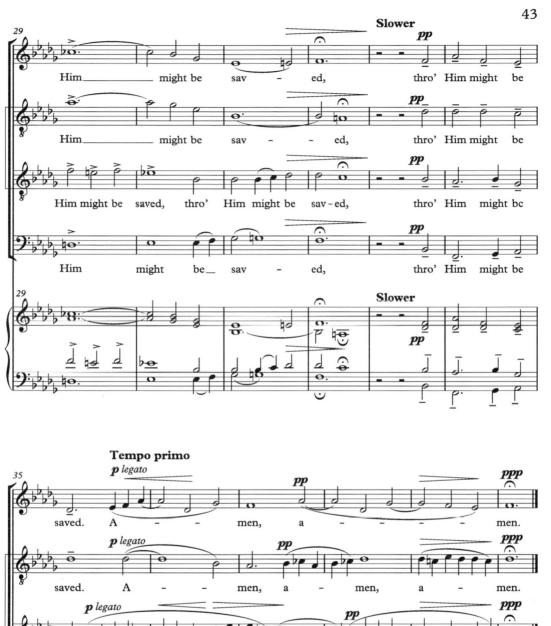

Grace

Psalm 115, v.1

Edward German

May be sung a semitone higher.

© Copyright 1921 Novello & Company Limited

To the memory of Evelyn Mary Ley

Holy is the true light

Words from *The Salisbury Diurnal*
by Dr. G. H. Palmer

William H. Harris

Baritones might perhaps sing with Tenor II when the notes are within their compass.
Original version for S.A.T.B.

© Copyright 1959 Novello & Company Limited

To Walter Parratt

I will lift up mine eyes

Psalm 121, vv.1-4

Ernest Walker, Op.16, No.1

© Copyright 1947 Novello & Company Limited

will lift up mine eyes un – to the hills:

p

(Ped.)

from whence__ com – eth my help.

f

f

f

p

My_ help com-eth e-ven from the Lord: who hath

made heaven and earth.

He will not suf-fer thy foot to be mov - ed:

He will not suf-fer thy

he that keep-eth Is - ra - el shall nei - ther

slum - ber nor sleep.

calando

calando

pp

pp

più dim.

ppp

If ye love me

John 14, vv.15-17

Thomas Tallis
ed. Barry Rose

© Copyright 2002 Novello & Company Limited

* pronounce sp'rit

In manus tuas

Responsory from the
office of Compline

John Sheppard
ed. Barry Rose

© Copyright 2002 Novello & Company Limited

Into thy hands, O Lord, I commend my spirit. For thou Lord, God of truth, hast redeemed me.

In paradisum
(Nunc dimittis)

IP: antiphon from the office of the Burial of the Dead
ND: from the office of Evensong in the Book of Common Prayer

E.W. Naylor

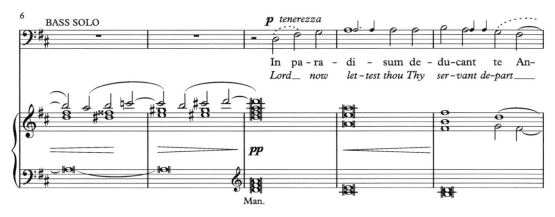

This work was first sung in the Chapel of Emmanuel College, Cambridge, on August 10, 1914, in memory of about 130 men of H.M.S. Amphion, blown up off Harwich by a German mine.

* Tutti ad lib.

64

E.W. Naylor also wrote a companion setting of the Magnificat in D major for lower voices.

Jubilate Deo

Psalm 100

Charles Macpherson

© Copyright 1911 Novello & Company Limited

Look down, O Lord

William Leighton (d.c.1616)
from *Teares or Lamentacions of a Sorrowful Soule*

William Byrd
ed. David Wulstan

© Copyright 1971 Chester Music Ltd.

Magnificat and Nunc Dimittis

MAGNIFICAT

Robin Doveton
(1973)

© Copyright 2002 Robin Doveton

attacca Gloria

GLORIA

NUNC DIMITTIS

Magnificat and Nunc Dimittis

MAGNIFICAT

Herbert Sumsion

© Copyright 1953 Novello & Company Limited
© renewed 1981

NUNC DIMITTIS

For the Chapel Choir of Christ's College, Cambridge

Oculi omnium

Psalm 145, v.15

Andrew Parnell

© Copyright 2002 Novello & Company Limited

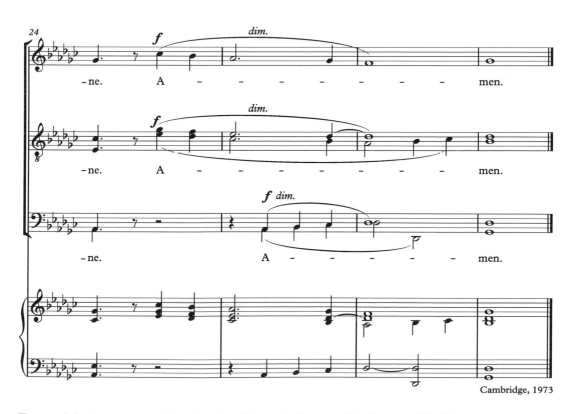

Cambridge, 1973

The eyes of all wait upon thee; and thou givest them their meat in due season. Glory be to thee O Lord. Amen.

O most merciful

Bishop Reginald Heber

Ernest Bullock

© Copyright 1938 Novello & Company Limited

* originally scored for TTBB

For the Gentlemen of Guildford Cathedral Choir

O praise God in his holiness

Psalm 150

Andrew Millington

The accompaniment was originally scored for brass quintet.

© Copyright 2002 Novello & Company Limited

great - ness.

Praise him in the sound of the trum - pet,

trum - pet: Praise him up - on the lute and harp.

Man.

Ped.

Praise him in the cym-bals and dan - ces: Praise him up-on the strings and pipe. Praise

Man.

Ped.

him up - on the well - tuned cym - bals:

Man.

Praise him up - on the loud

cym - bals. Let e - v'ry - thing that hath breath:

Man.

Ped.

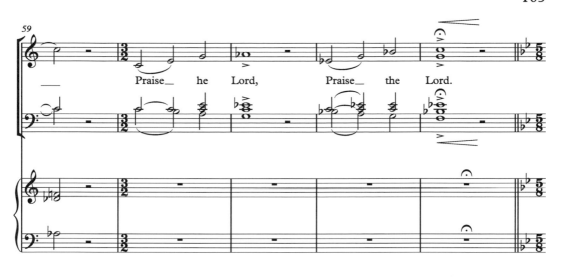

Praise_ he Lord, Praise_ the Lord.

Glo - ry

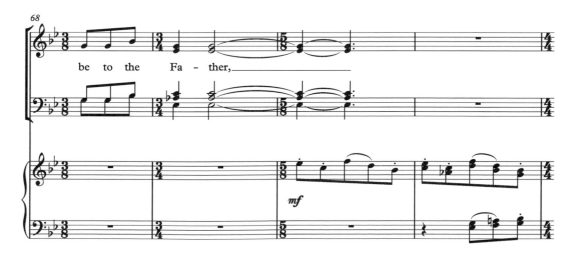

be to the Fa - ther,_____

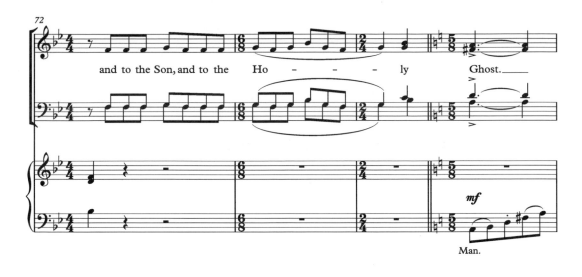

and to the Son, and to the Ho - - - ly Ghost.___

Man.

As it was in the be - gin - ning, is

Ped.

now_ and e - ver shall be, world with - out

Preces and Responses

Stephen Cleobury

THE PRECES

© Copyright 2002 Novello & Company Limited

Praise ye the Lord. The Lord's name be praised.

THE RESPONSES

The Lord be with you.

And with thy spi - rit.

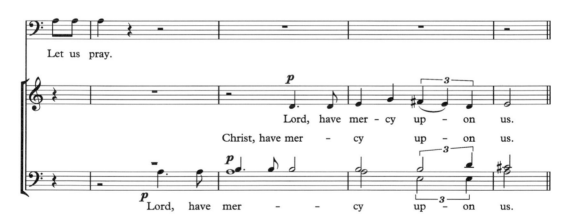

Let us pray.

Lord, have mer - cy up - on us.

Christ, have mer - cy up - on us.

Lord, have mer - cy up - on us.

Our Father.

Our Father... but deliver us from e-vil, A - men.

O Lord, shew thy mer-cy up - on us.

And grant us thy sal - va - tion.

O Lord, save the Queen.

And mer-ci-ful-ly hear us___ when we call up-on thee.

And mer-ci-ful-ly hear___ us when we call up-on thee.

Endue thy ministers with right-eous-ness.

And make thy cho - sen peo - ple joy - ful.

O Lord, save thy peo-ple.

And bless___ thine in - he - ri -tance.

THE COLLECTS

If there is a 4th Collect, repeat 1st Amen.

FINAL RESPONSES

Ferial

The Lord be with you

And with thy spi – rit.

The Lord give us his peace.

And life e – ter – nal, A – men.

Festal

The Lord be with you

And with thy spi – rit.

Let us bless the Lord.

Thanks be to God.

Salve Regina

Antiphon from the
office of Compline

Christopher Tye
ed. Barry Rose

© Copyright 2002 Novello & Company Limited

Hail, Queen, mother of pity! Our life, sweetness, and hope, hail! To thee we cry, the exiled sons of Eve. To thee we sigh, lamenting and weeping in this valley of tears.

Sancta Maria

Text anon.

John Dunstable
ed. Barry Rose

© Copyright 2002 Novello & Company Limited

118

Holy Mary, in this world there has arisen none like thee among women.
Blooming like the rose, fragrant as the lily, pray for us, holy Mother of God.

To Ernest Mills

The shepherds' farewell
from *The Childhood of Christ*

Hector Berlioz,
tr. Paul England

Hector Berlioz,
arr. K.J. Dinham

© Copyright 1973 Novello & Company Limited

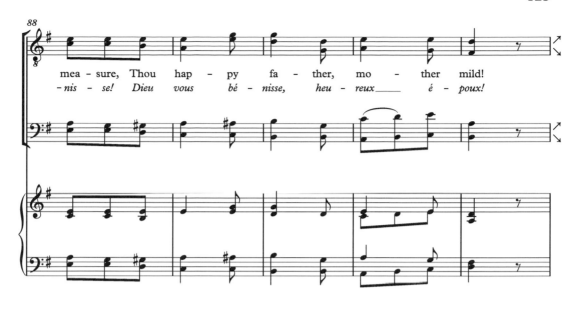

mea - sure, Thou hap - py fa - ther, mo - ther mild!
-nis - se! Dieu vous bé - nisse, heu - reux____ é - poux!

Guard ye well your Heav'n - ly Trea - sure, The Prince of Peace, the
Que ja - mais de l'in - jus - ti - ce Vous ne puis - siez sen -

Guard ye well your Heav'n-ly Trea - sure, The__ Prince of__ Peace, the
Que ja - mais de l'in-jus - ti - ce Vous__ ne puis - siez sen -

Guard ye well your Heav'n - ly Trea - sure, The Prince of Peace, the
Que ja - mais de l'in - jus - ti - ce Vous ne puis - siez sen -

Guard ye well your Heav'n - ly Trea - sure, The Prince__ of Peace,__ the
Que ja - mais de l'in - jus - ti - ce Vous ne__ puis - siez__ sen -

Sicut cervus

Psalm 42, v.1

G.P. da Palestrina
ed. Anthony G. Petti

© Copyright 1977 J. & W. Chester/Edition Wilhelm Hansen London Ltd.
This edtion © Copyright 2002 Chester Music Limited

As the hart longs for water, so my soul yearns for you, O God.

Thou, O God, art praised in Sion

Psalm 65, vv.1-2

Charles Macpherson

© Copyright 1920 Novello & Company Limited

and un – to Thee shall the vow be per – form – ed____

and un – to Thee____ shall the vow__ be per – form – ed____

Thee,____ un – to Thee shall the vow__ be per – form – ed____

____ in____ Je – ru – sa – lem.____

– ru – sa – lem.____

____ in____ Je – ru – sa – lem.____

____ in____ Je – ru – sa – lem.____

Gt.

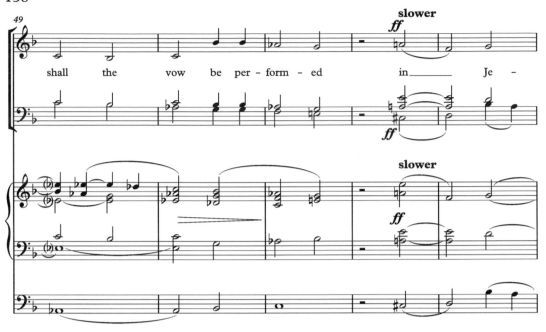

shall the vow be per-form-ed in _____ Je-

-ru - sa-lem.

Upon this Holy Eastertide

In dieser österlichen Zeit

Ludwig Helmbold,
tr. Maurice Bevan

Johannes Eccard
arr. Maurice Bevan

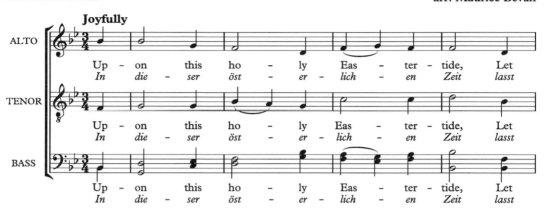

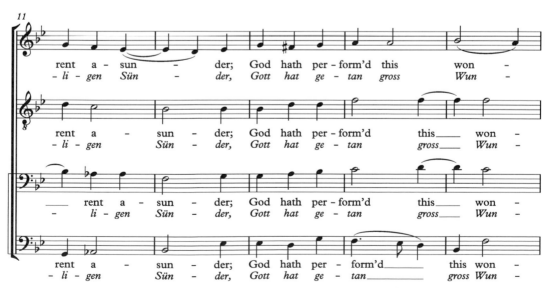

© Copyright 2002 Novello & Company Limited

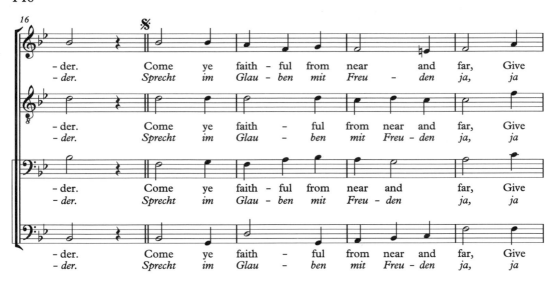

When Christ was born of Mary free

15th century

John Joubert

No. 4 of Five Carols, op. 78

This version © Copyright 2002 Novello & Company Limited

fair ci - ty, An - gels sung e'er with mirth and glee, In___ ex - cel - sis,

fair ci - ty, An - gels sung e'er with mirth and glee, In___ ex - cel - sis,

fair ci - ty, An - gels sung e'er with mirth and glee, In___ ex - cel - sis,

in___ ex - cel - sis, in___ ex - cel - sis glo - ri - a.___

in___ ex - cel - sis, in___ ex - cel - sis glo - ri - a.___

in___ ex - cel - sis, in___ ex - cel - sis glo - ri - a.___

2. Herds - men be - held these an - gels bright – To them ap - pear - ed